B Kliban®

catchristmas

Pomegranate

SAN FRANCISCO

Published by Pomegranate Communications, Inc.
Box 808022, Petaluma CA 94975
800 277 1428; www.pomegranate.com

Pomegranate Europe Ltd.
Unit 1, Heathcote Business Centre, Hurlbutt Road
Warwick, Warwickshire CV34 6TD, UK
[+44] 0 1926 430111; sales@pomeurope.co.uk

© 2002 Judith Kamman Kliban
www.eatmousies.com
www.kliban.com
Lyrics © 2002 Pomegranate Communications, Inc.

All rights reserved.

No part of this publication may be reproduced or transmitted in any form
or by any means, electronic or mechanical, including photocopying, or by any
information storage or retrieval system, without permission in writing from
the copyright holders.

Library of Congress Control Number: 2002104404

ISBN 978-0-7649-2108-7
Pomegranate Catalog No. A634
Printed in China

19 18 17 16 15 14 13 12 11 10   13 12 11 10 9 8 7 6 5 4

Cats

As far as I know, cats were invented a few hundred years ago by some Egyptians, who noticed that they had the word 'cat' (or 'qat⁺') in their language without anything to stick it on. The invention of cats (qats) filled in the gap nicely and the cat was off to a running start, as it were.

The cat would have remained just sort of a Teddy-type animal had it not been for the addition of tiny fangs and claws around the time of the Civil War, on the same principle that a handful of jalapeños will perk up the morning oatmeal, or at least help it to catch mice.

After their perfection in 1935 (fatter

Tails, more ears) they rapidly became an important factor in the growth of the cat food industry, a mainstay of our western democratic culture.

An interesting fact about cats is that they will absolutely not do anything they don't want to, unlike us and dogs. Now consider this chart of cat advantages.

	DOG	FISH	BIRD	FRUIT	CAT
MEOWING			✓		✓
CLIMBING					✓
PURRING					✓
CATCHING BUGS			✓		✓
WASHING FACE		✓			✓
NON-BARKING					✓

I hope this has helped you to appreciate and understand cats a little more, so the next time you run into one, let him make you take him to lunch

BKliban

B. "Hap" Kliban (1935–1990) rocked the world of funny-animal cartooning with his wonderfully quirky images of Cat. A serious artist who first studied painting and design at Pratt Institute and Cooper Union, Kliban lived for a time in Europe, drawing incessantly and perfecting a talent for figure drawing. Returning to the United States, he worked a number of odd (!) jobs in San Francisco. One of these was a gig at the Mr. Wonderful Club, drawing the showgirls there. Between portraits of exotic dancers, Kliban drew bitingly hilarious cartoons on cocktail napkins.

In 1962, Kliban answered an ad in *Playboy* for contributions from cartoonists, and a thirty-year relationship with that magazine was born. During the early 1970s, Kliban—a cat lover—idly drew his four resident felines as he contemplated ideas for *Playboy*. Those drawings found their way to a literary agent, who cut a deal with a publisher, and so in 1975 Cat stalked onto the scene. Kliban became a cartoon sensation, producing such maniacally funny books as *Whack Your Porcupine* and *The Biggest Tongue in Tunisia*.

Cat and his colorful cousins may be the best remembered of Kliban's characters; today they are still adored icons and trusted friends, beloved by all who sense a connection with their delightfully strange worldview.

Note: The lyrics to the Christmas carols presented in this book were written by hitherto unknown writers, all inspired by Hap Kliban's art. Hap didn't know any of them.

Oh Christmas Tree, Oh Christmas Tree

Your ornaments make great toys

Oh Christmas Tree, Oh Christmas Tree

Your tinsel brings us great joys

Your star on top is hard to get

But give us time, we'll get it yet

Oh Christmas Tree, Oh Christmas Tree

Please stay all year we love you.

—Lyrics by Oscar Beany Catt (1983-1995)

9

10

We wish you a mousie Christmas

We wish you a mousie Christmas

We wish you a mousie Christmas

And a fishy New Year!

Good scratchings we brings

To you and your things

We wish you a mousie Christmas

And a fishy New Year!

—Lyrics by Salmon D. Fishdie (b. *1993*)

14

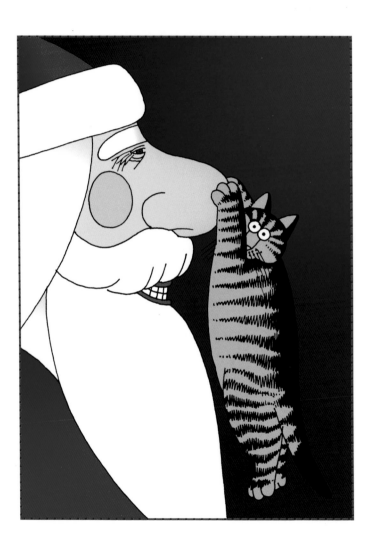

Hark the hungry kitties sing

"Give us kitties everything!

Sushi, mousies, milk and cheese

Don't expect us to say please!

Hear us yowl for lots of treats

Fish and fowl, fresh—cut meats

With some ice cream don't forget!

We've always been your favorite pets!"

Hark the hungry kitties sing

"Give us kitties everything!"

—Lyrics by Kit McPaw

(1967–1978)

Kitties we have heard on high
Slyly watching o'er the house
Patiently with beady eye
Waiting for a tasty mouse

Oh, Taa-stee Mouse,
Taa-stee Mouse
Taa-stee Mouse we want
Then we'll go to sleep
Oh, Taa-stee Mouse,
Taa-stee Mouse
Taa-stee Mouse we want
Then we'll go to sleep

—Lyrics by Foggy Catfeet (b. 1994)

the twelve days of christmas

On the first day of Christmas
my kitty gave to me
A hairball under my tree.

On the second day of Christmas
my kitty gave to me
Two dead mice
And a hairball under my tree.

On the third day of Christmas
my kitty gave to me
Three head nibbles
Two dead mice
And a hairball under my tree.

On the fourth day of Christmas
my kitty gave to me
Four chewed pens
Three head nibbles
Two dead mice
And a hairball under my tree.

On the fifth day of Christmas
my kitty gave to me
Five dead birds
Four chewed pens
Three head nibbles
Two dead mice
And a hairball under my tree.

On the sixth day of Christmas
my kitty gave to me
Six ankle rubs
Five dead birds
Four chewed pens
Three head nibbles
Two dead mice
And a hairball under my tree.

On the seventh day of Christmas
my kitty gave to me
Seven leaping fleas
Six ankle rubs
Five dead birds
Four chewed pens
Three head nibbles
Two dead mice
And a hairball under my tree.

On the eighth day of Christmas
my kitty gave to me
Eight armchair scratches
Seven leaping fleas
Six ankle rubs
Five dead birds
Four chewed pens
Three head nibbles
Two dead mice
And a hairball under my tree.

On the ninth day of Christmas
my kitty gave to me
Nine feet of ribbon
Eight armchair scratches
Seven leaping fleas
Six ankle rubs
Five dead birds
Four broken pens
Three head nibbles
Two dead mice
And a hairball under my tree.

On the tenth day of Christmas
my kitty gave to me
Ten chewed shoelaces
Nine feet of ribbon
Eight armchair scratches
Seven leaping fleas
Six ankle rubs
Five dead birds
Four broken pens
Three head nibbles
Two dead mice
And a hairball under my tree.

On the eleventh day of Christmas
my kitty gave to me
Eleven matted furballs
Ten chewed shoelaces
Nine feet of ribbon

Eight armchair scratches
Seven leaping fleas
Six ankle rubs
Five dead birds
Four broken pens
Three head nibbles
Two dead mice
And a hairball under my tree.

On the twelfth day of Christmas
my kitty gave to me
Twelve minutes of purrs
Eleven matted furballs
Ten chewed shoelaces
Nine feet of ribbon
Eight armchair scratches
Seven leaping fleas
Six ankle rubs
Five dead birds
Four broken pens
Three head nibbles
Two dead mice
And a hairball under
my tree.

—Lyrics by S. "Nose"
Scratch (1959-1972)

30

jinglebells

Jingle Bells, Jingle Bells
Jingle all the way
Oh what fun it is to hide
Underneath the Chevrolet, Hey!
Jingle Bells, Jingle Bells
Jingle all the way
How we love to be the pets
Who always disobey!

Dashing through the house
As we chase each other 'round
Scratching on the chair
And eating stuff we've found
Making lots of noise
At midnight is the best
And when the people go away
Is when we get our rest, Oh!

[repeat chorus]

—Lyrics by Earl "Tiger" Heeaynt (b. 1990)

38

thelittledrumstickcat

*C*ome, they told me,
Pa rumpa pum pum
A new-baked bird you see
Pa rumpa pum pum
It's in the oven there
Pa rumpa pum pum
We offer you a dare
Pa rumpa pum pum
Rumpa pum pum
Rumpa pum pum
Steal a drumstick
Pa rumpa pum pum
And a plum.

So I waited
Pa rumpa pum pum
My breath was bated
Pa rumpa pum pum
At last the bird was done
Pa rumpa pum pum
My time to act had come
Pa rumpa pum pum

Rumpa pum pum
Rumpa pum pum
So I wrangled it
Pa rumpa pum pum
And a plum.

All my kitty chums
Pa rumpa pum pum
They watched and cheered me on
Pa rumpa pum pum
They have their drumstick now
Pa rumpa pum pum
They have their sweet plum now
Pa rumpa pum pum
Rumpa pum pum
Rumpa pum pum
Then I had a bite
Pa rumpa pum pum
Yum yum yum.

—Lyrics by Wheela Brie (b. 1999)

44

Joy to the Cat!
For now he's home
We don't know where he's been!
He hid somewhere for days
And now he wants our praise
And rubs behind his ears
And rubs behind his ears
And rubs, and rubs behind his ears.

He rules the world!
And we obey
We give him what he wants!
He sleeps all afternoon
He yowls out of tune
It's music to our ears
It's music to our ears
It's music, it's music to our ears.

—Lyrics by Sushi Herringway (b. 1997)

47

48